Wedding

Decoration

Ideas

By

Pairs Kay Hersom

Wedding Decoration Ideas

By Paris Kay Hersom

© Copyright 2013 Paris Kay Hersom

First Published, 2013

Printed in the United States of America

Five Star Reviews!

*"**Such Romantic Ideas** - Really creative and imaginative ideas that could also be used for decorating ideas for other parties. Very nice pictures and beautiful suggestions to make the day very special. Lots of inexpensive decorations as well!"*

*"**Elegent decorating ideas!** - We all need decorating ideas from time to time. But if you are planning a wedding, reception or cocktail party, I recommend this book. The author has some wonderful ideas, unique and certainly different - with elegance! Great idea book!"*

*"**This book is packed with helpful wedding decoration ideas!** -* Anyone seeking information about wedding decoration ideas could definitely benefit from reading this book. Not only does it contain helpful decoration ideas, but there's also a lot of beautiful pictures that compliment many of decoration ideas provided. This is an excellent wedding book, well worth reading if you're planning a wedding in the near future..."

Table of Contents

Wedding Decoration Ideas

The Moment

Two lives joined together...Two hearts that beat as one...And the moment of blush when you promise saying "I Do!" The man and woman pledge to live in love forever! Your Wedding day truly is a blissful occasion filled with joy, hope and dreams. The ambience and decoration will surely add to this ecstatic moment since these are the most memorable moments which are going to be captured and cherished for a lifetime! Be it a large gathering or a small get together, we all take pride in making happy, our friends and relatives who have come to wish everlasting happiness and bless our wedding. So the following are a few decoration ideas, which will add to the glamour of your wedding day making you look more beautiful and your guests all the more pleased!

"Wedding Reception Decoration" A Few Easy Tips for a Great Day!

Time to Light It Up

The color white denotes peace and tranquility; therefore white Christmas lights are an awesome addition to any wedding reception. Used with tulle they can be hung around the cake table, around the reception tables, in potted plants, in arch ways and from the ceiling. Simply put, just light it up. It's hard to overdo it with tulle and lighting.

Tie Ribbons

Ribbons make the celebration look like a royal event! Therefore, wide ribbons can be tied in a bow at the back of your chair as they look elegant and beautiful. One of the best things about ribbons is that they are cheap alternatives to fancy seat covers. Red and White color ribbon combination would give an awesome look!

Water Fountain

Who does not love places with water? It totally transforms our mood and keeps us pleasant. A water fountain at the entrance of the reception would be a wonderful way to welcome our guests. Few fountains with lights, near the tables would also be a great idea.

Chocolate Fountain

Need we say anymore than that people LOVE chocolate!

Feathers

Feathers signify smoothness and light-heartedness! They look both trendy and traditional in the wedding decoration. Feather wreaths can be hung on walls for a very cozy and decorative look!

Ice Carvings

Nothing shouts out elegancy has much as a good ice carving can. This should be one of your wedding signature pieces and be placed in an area of attraction for optimum effect and display. The carving should be theme in line with your overall wedding theme too and/or also be a functional piece and not just for show. For example have the sculpture created in the shape of a wine rack and put wine bottles in it for chilling and to be served from ice carving display.

Food Decoration

Finally guests would love to savor the food items. In your wedding reception, you can decorate the food to add excitement to your big day! Desserts are always the most awaited ones…So create the festive mood you want, by placing apothecary jars full of candy on every dessert bar. Or have carved fruit in different wedding theme shapes placed around the banquet tables.

Centerpiece Ideas

The wedding centerpieces are meant to make all the tables in a given room distinctive while enhancing the overall wedding decorations. Regardless of the price, the wedding centerpiece should be good looking and appealing. Worried about wedding centerpiece ideas? Well, here are some affordable wedding centerpiece ideas you may want to consider.

Martini Glass Centerpiece

Fill a martini glass with water and then float a smaller sized candle inside it. It is possible to liven it up further through the addition of color to the water and then tying a colorful and bright ribbon to the stem.

Good Ole Glass Bowl

Use pebbles or colorful beads in filling the base, and put in the flowers and candles. The other option takes more time but is unique. Acquire small and colorful Styrofoam balls and then try slitting them at their center. Have these materials placed near the bowl's rim. It is possible to use one color if you don't want the centerpiece to become too colorful.

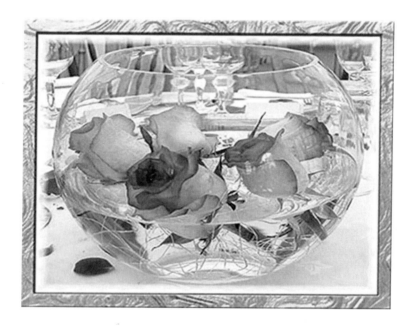

Cute and Personal Centerpiece

Paint over slender and tall pots or tall and old tins. For every pot, write a distinctive personal message and ensure the two of you sign it, as you thank every guest for making the wedding day rather special through their attendance and in sharing your happiness.

Curly Willow Centerpiece

The curly willow branches make appealing centerpieces. They can add height to your centerpiece, making the overall décor interesting. You can do this in an elaborate or a simple way.

Shocking Centerpiece

One may also add jazz to a cheap centerpiece. Simply pick up the dried and old leaves from the yard. Spray paint the leaves in your preferred metallic color or combined colors. Place these on a flat plate with some small tea-lights. Light from your candles highlights the leaves, thereby giving the centerpiece an ultimate jazz.

Shells by the Seashore

Shells can be used in centerpieces or as the centerpiece itself, and at a very low cost. Shells bring unique, but natural look and feel especially if your wedding is near the beach, it will be the right prop!

Candles

Candles are the most romantic way of expressing love and there is none who does not like it! Dim rooms lit with the glow of candles are just amazing and can be purchased ahead of time at little expense. Use them in centerpieces on the receptions tables.

Fabrics

Fabric decoration is one unique way to embellish on your reception day! Use fabrics to create an intimate atmosphere and use them to cover the tables or to add highlights of your wedding colors. Weave colored fabric throughout your serving and cake tables too.

Picnic

If you are doing an outdoor or beach wedding you may want to go with a modified picnic theme for your guests. Your wedding "tables" can be used along with pillows and blankets on the ground, each one of them with its own basket of picnic items in line with your wedding theme.

Wedding Ceremony Decoration

Planning the Where

Indoor wedding or outdoor wedding? Outdoor weddings and especially beach weddings have been growing in popularity over the last decade. If an outdoor venue is chosen always make sure to book an indoor back up plan. Never assume that mister sunshine will be shining on your special day. Make sure in advance about the scope of decorations allowed at your wedding venue location. If you are going to get married at the beach or in a church, find out what they can provide to help in the area of decorations. Some facilities have some standard decorations that could be useful to your own wedding theme.

Church Bells Are Ringing

Church wedding decorations are interesting since you need them to look unique while you still maintain the sacred nature of the church. The church wedding decorations are done to give the guests a different feel from when they are attending a normal church service. Some of the outstanding decorations mainly involve decorating using flowers, candles and white decor. The best approach to doing this form of decoration is doing it by location as follows.

Church Entrance

The entrance of the church should be decorated with floral arrangements and/or a floral design on either side of the rails at the church entrance. Eye catching flowers to signify that this is a special day at the church.

Down the Aisle

For a beautiful setting hang tulle and flowers from each wooden pew of the church aisle. Decorations should be designed to have a floral design at the neck of the wood and then the bottom part of the draping should flow slightly onto the carpet of the aisle. If the seats are plastic and standalone units, you can get white seat covers for every seat. You can tie another piece of cloth on the backrest of the seat. This cloth should match the theme of the wedding.

It is important to get a carpet runner that complements the color of the carpet, white or red are some of the most common colors. The carpet runner can also make it easy to clear the flowers after the guests leave the church for the reception if you decide to place rose petals down the aisle to the altar.

The Church Front

The table located at the center front section of the church which sometimes may be used for communion or placing a Unity candle, this table should be decorated with a long white table cloth and a top cloth that matches the wedding theme color. Fresh flowers in a vase may be placed on either side of the table. Candles on the table and a floral arch where the pews end also add style and fare to the church wedding decor.

Nature Has Its Own Cathedral

Outdoor weddings can offer the most spectacular settings in nature's own cathedral whether it is a sandy beach, lush flower garden or a mountain ridge backdrop. Outdoor weddings have almost all the decoration you need. Getting married in spring is a good idea, since all the flowers are in their full bloom and it will be the most colorful garden wedding.

Tulle It Up

Tulle is a good way to create a canopy effect using lots of tulles. They can also be used on the rows of chairs to add more effect. The couple should always be highlighted so that they look special and all the guests have a good look at them. There must be a focal point for the couple and arches and gazebos are the best for it! Again tulle is beautiful way to decorate either one to look elegant. Then add a few flowers for accent.

Don't Forget the Candles

Just because you are outside don't forget the candles to set the romantic mood. Candles are the romantic touch which you need at your wedding ceremony. They may be placed beside flower arrangements, even in the bouquets, and at the altar to beautify.

A Touch of Green

Potted plants can add a touch of green elegance even to an outdoor setting. The natural garden atmosphere can be created by using potted plants on the aisle or at the altar area.

Time to Runner Up

Yes we are outside, but don't forget the carpet runner, it will add so much. Especially when sprinkled with flower petals. Nothing is more beautiful than decorating the place with flower petals on the aisle before your guests arrive. It will surely make them feel special.

Creative Juices

I hope your creative juices are now flowing with inspired wedding decoration ideas and may the wedding you're planning be wonderful!

God Bless,

Paris Kay Hersom

Resources

To find most of the wedding centerpieces, favors and more talked about in my book

http://click.linksynergy.com/fs-bin/click?id=6Lxess0Uh38&offerid=211726&type=3&subid=0

More Wedding Ideas

Like to keep your creative wedding decoration inspiration up, then you'll love this wedding book by Paris Kay Hersom.

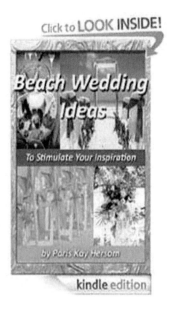

Beach Wedding Ideas available on Amazon Kindle and paperback.

Enjoyed the Book?

Thank You for Buying This Book. I was hoping you could help your fellow book enthusiasts out and when you have a free second leave you honest feedback about this book. I certainly want to thank you in advance for doing this.

Made in United States
North Haven, CT
29 June 2022

20755858R00015